DEAD REDHEAD

TRACEY HERD

DEAD REDHEAD

BLOODAXE BOOKS

ISBN: 1 85224 565 4

First published 2001 by
Bloodaxe Books Ltd,
Highgreen,
Tarset,
Northumberland NE48 1RP.

Bloodaxe Books Ltd acknowledges
the financial assistance of Northern Arts.

Cover printing by J. Thomson Colour Printers Ltd, Glasgow.

Printed in Great Britain by
Cromwell Press Ltd, Trowbridge, Wiltshire.

For Dave,
Ian and Isla

Acknowledgements

Acknowledgements are due to the editors of the following publications in which some of these poems first appeared: *Kenyon Review, Inkpellet, Last Words* (Picador, 1999), *Love for Love* (Pocketbooks/ Morning Star Publications, 2000), *New Blood* (Bloodaxe Books, 1999), *Red Wheelbarrow, Shore Poets Anthology* (2001), *Stand* and *Verse*.

The protagonist of the sequence *The Mystery of the Missing Century* is based on Carolyn Keene's girl detective Nancy Drew, but displaced into a murder fiction whose characters include many contemporary female cultural icons.

I am grateful to the University of Dundee and the Scottish Arts Council for a creative writing fellowship in 1998-2001 and to the British Council for inviting me to take part in the British Council/ Bloodaxe Poetry Festival events in Moscow and Ekaterinburg in 1998, and special thanks are due to Dr Victor Skretkowicz, Dr Ian Francis, Sasha Dugdale, Alla Onishchenko and Galina Nesterenko.

Contents

I watched the couple I could see, the curse
And blessings of that couple, their destination,
The deception practised on them at the station,
The courage. When the train stopped and they knew
The end of their journey, I descended too.

JOHN BERRYMAN
The Traveller

A Letter from Anna

I tiptoe the distance from the bedroom door
across the thickly carpeted, cream-coloured floor.
I might be crossing a country or a mountain stream
but I have travelled further for much less
and for you I would travel barefoot
through the pine forests covered by snow and ice.

Although practical in every other sense,
I have lost my heart to you, my love; and I
even with my dark dreams of death
have thoughts like small night-fires
to warm my freezing fingers by, now unadorned
by the thin gold band and the vows I made
to my husband to be faithful, and a good wife.

I no longer dance gracefully at parties, flirting
thoughtlessly in my small-waisted flaring dresses
and make small-talk with the select list of guests.
I am no longer welcome at their grand palaces
and my gems lie dully in their velvet-lined box:
the emeralds are flowers shrouded in winter
and my diamonds are grey in a storm-burdened sky.
Only the rubies are bright, and that is an ill omen.
Now I will tell you our story as I wish it had happened.

Your beautiful mare would never have fallen, she'd
have finished the steeplechase at the head
of a procession, every bone in her body unbroken
and now, she'd be grazing the paddock with her colt
by her side. For me, there would be no walk
to the station, no pause in the shadows away
from the lanterns, and no departure, with the great
black train's wheels in slow motion as I fell forward
into the oil-stained tracks. We'd be lying here,
under white covers, two children lost in the benevolent
forest, clutching each other to stave off the cold
and patiently waiting for a Russian spring.

Big Red

I am the horse-mad girl whose dreams went up in smoke
but sometimes my mind will unwrap a horse's silks
and I have my vast dirt-tracks and racing stables.
In 1973, I steered the big red horse, faster, double, triple
until the runner-up was beyond any tilted camera angle
and the track was churning and the breathless crowds

broke into frenzied cheering and the betting slips
went up in flames just like the colour of his coat.
He had barely broken sweat but I was shaking
and he stood there in the circle, a god of his own making
as the others trailed unnoticed by the post.
At nineteen, the huge bronzed horse took his final turn

from the stables to the graveyard at Claiborne Farms.
Not just his hooves and heart and head went into the ground
but the whole horse was lowered gently down
for some things on this earth deserve such preservation
and his heart was twice as heavy, pound for pound,
as any other horse's, and his name I still conjure like a charm.

Secretariat. Big Red. That Triple Crown.
I circle the bronze marker in the ground
and let my fingers tighten round the roughness of his mane.

Edie
(for Jo)

Two friends held an impromptu wake for me in a New York bar,
ordered their drinks, lit up, and placed a cigarette for me, balanced
on the curved glass rim of an ashtray and shared their memories
and twenty minutes later, the cigarette began to glow, and smoke
curled sweetly into the air, they said, and one murmured, Edie's here.
Poor fools. I'd been dead for days, cold, without breath, no lungs left
to inhale or exhale one last cigarette. I'd left my glittering life
and died my mundane death. How could I possibly be there?
And they were unpacking and shaking out so many years, back to
        The Factory,
my dangling shoulder-skimming earrings and my cropped platinum hair
and maybe somewhere the dresses are still limp and silver on their
        hangers,
my black tights and my leotards tossed across someone's bed,
and false lashes and the bright gold powder smudged with fingermarks
but Edie's gone, my dear old friends, gone far away, and I'm sleeping
now just like a little baby and you can come and see the metal plate
pushed into the ground: Edith Sedgewick Post. 1943-71.
The music's stopped, I'm out of touch, the party's over.
The invitations lie unopened on their silver salver. Platinum queen,
poor little rich girl, dancing into the early hours. I've kicked off
my high heels, with relief, and stretched out my long, long legs
on my queen-sized, canopied silk bed. I've finally gone home
back to my mad father and all the illustrious Sedgewick clan,
my two dear brothers who bowed out too young. Someone else's
cigarette must have brushed the unlit one. I would have appreciated
your lovely thoughts, but no, I didn't come.

The Water Babies

Each night, Joan Crawford would tie her red hair back
from her smooth forehead with a bandeau,
scooping out the cold-cream
from a white porcelain jar, to cleanse
her skin of the foundation and thick powder
then she'd scowl at her freckles
and rub her face with ice-cubes till it stung.

Marilyn would buy a new pair of jeans,
wriggling her hips into the stiff blue denim
then lie in a cold bath for hours
till they'd shrunk to fit her
like a second skin. But still her skin
was too thin. Her hair was mousy then,
streaming down her back in unruly curls.
She lifted weights, she ran the back alleys of Hollywood.
She loved the sea, would swim with powerful strokes
out far from shore: she'd parade in a pink swimsuit
twirling a parasol, leaning down to sketch
names in the sand and smile her smile
till they taught her to pull her lips down over her gums.
When George Barris took the final shots,
she wrapped herself in a Mexican-knit cardigan
against the mist, her hair clumped, her face
pasty and dry, her eyes cast down
looking for the lost names in the sand.

Natalie Wood's brown eyes and chestnut hair,
her journals of life's small joys, her mediocre
acting skills that didn't matter when you looked
at *that* face, drowned in a boating accident
off Catalina, no witnesses, no saviour,
her lungs filled with the stars reflected in the dark
Pacific. There was no poor dialogue to spoil the scene,
just the doe-eyed beauty, mute and pale, her body
lit from within by tiny stars.

Anne Sexton's Last Letter to God

This is the last letter I will write
sitting at my kitchen table
with the blue coffee mug
at my elbow and the pot
roasting each bean to perfection:
faraway continents
in my cluttered suburban kitchen.
The sun is sharp through the blinds,
crisscrossing the kitchen's
clean tiles with yellow and white.
I walk a knife-edge of light.
This is the last letter I will write.

I have been a witch, clothed in rags
and shrieking. I have borrowed
the wings of angels and given them back:
a poor fit, and yes, like Icarus
I had no sense and I didn't much like
falling back to earth. I have had lovers
by the dozen, some poets and others
and a faithful husband that I left
in the end. I have written painfully evocative
letters from Europe and many poems,
but this is the last letter I will write.

God is in your typewriter, the old priest said
and I wanted a father so badly, that for months
I believed him, transfixed by small miracles
and clutching my golden crucifix
on my knees by the empty bed. Lately

I have given a few well-received readings
in my high heels and my favourite red dress,
the posters that displayed me in defiant pose.
I was always dramatic with my husky voice,
my fingers curled around a cigarette
and the ending always upbeat.
I have just lunched with an old friend
saying goodbye and something
'she couldn't quite catch'.

Now I have locked the front door behind me,
squinting a little as autumn spills down
from the skies and the trees. Here
is a small miracle and I am walking away.
I wrap my mother's fur coat
tightly around me, although I have
no need of its warmth today. The sun
is a cat stroking my neck, winding itself
contentedly around my long, slender legs.
I pause by the garage door to admire
the autumn leaves in their *sourball* colours.

A drink is in order. A double.
A toast to old friends, to those
on the other end of the phone and to those
who for one reason or another
have abandoned me. I pull the car door
closed and turn the key.
This, God, is *my* journey.
I have cut the lines
between us: no more tantrums.
No more poems. I am not
your daughter, your mother, your lover.
No more letters then, from me to you, God
and it amuses me to think of your
impotent displeasure as I settle myself
comfortably into the driver's seat.

Breakfast at Tiffanys
(for Carole)

> *There are only diamonds in the whole world,*
> *diamonds and perhaps the shabby gift of disillusion.*
> F. SCOTT FITZGERALD

Holly Golightly haunts the streets of New York.
Look into the distance. The girl is gone,
and each diamond is simply a star in the dark

that she followed far from the well-worn track.
Now the stars are her jewels, the night, her gown.
Holly Golightly haunts the streets of New York.

Her reflection was elegant, slender and stark.
She toasted each dawn by strolling downtown
to the diamonds that spilled like tears from the dark.

Her moon river still leaps like a cat over rocks,
her small voice floating its singular tune.
Holly Golightly haunts the streets of New York

slipping on shades to mimic the black
for she knew that the party would be over too soon
and that diamonds are lovely tricks of the dark

in each life, that solitary walk
into a distance that is ours alone.
Holly Golightly haunts the streets of New York,
and each diamond? Just a diamond, lost in the dark.

The First Blonde

Beneath the poster of Jean Harlow
(before uremic poisoning turned her yellow
as a farm-girl in the Kansas sun
stamping fields of brittle corn
till the dust had stained her skin),

I try to sleep, tangled in the cotton sheets
trashed with sweating cascades of flowers.
Voices crackle from the walls,
glasses break, a brazen girl laughs
and I want her here in taut white satin

with her lurid lips and nails, an
artificial angel in impossible heels
flaunting her tanned breasts, her nipples
rubbed with ice before each take,
no underwear, up close, her stinking breath.

Her mother killed her: no doctor
for the tired-eyed dentist's daughter, her hair
as whitely plastic as a doll's, dark roots
leaking over the grubby pillow, as mother
prays half-heartedly and her kidneys fail her.

Tickets are cheap. The rotting flowers are free
along the dusty road from Missouri westwards,
to *Saratoga*: the glowing blonde double
who doesn't speak, and from a distance
looks like her but isn't.

What Gentlemen Prefer

She had such beautiful and glamorous things.
SPOKESPERSON, CHRISTIES, NEW YORK

Not for sale, two lipsticks, red, used;
although the gold powder compact
with acceptance speech *tucked*
poignantly inside, is in the catalogue.
Who wants the dried-up glycerine
and wax her lips had touched?
What weird alchemy might she
have worked, and who really wants
what she had? That neediness,
the hair like straw, the gold
lamé dress so tight that
she had to be stitched into it;
the mad, knife-wielding mother,
the abortions, the phone-calls
at 2 a.m. to fed-up friends:
I can't sleep. Please come over.
That spilling out. *Every girl*
needs a da-da-daddy. Men
only love happy girls. All
she had to do was smile,
be punctual and read the script.
It wasn't that difficult. *Hollywood*
Cinderella girl, a fire-escape,
iron spirals, thin spike heels,
wisps of artificial smoke for hair,
the hem of her white, pleated dress
fleeing upwards from her ankles
in the rush down to the flames,
right profile turned towards the camera:
a merry girl, impetuous but dumb,
burned alive and radiantly blonde.

Stone Angel

(for Isobel)

Stone angels in a Roman spring. No, make that summer:
A breathless afternoon in the kingdom of earth,
the dust rising in columns of silence to smother

the girl who is kneeling, sweet bird of youth,
in her loose white dress that skims slim ankles
at the temple of her father and her sweat-soaked faith.

His silence is thick with summer and smoke. Baby doll.
The sunlight strokes her spine with thin, hot fingers
as she pulls at roots and a fountain of petals

that she brushes from her palms, the ruins of summer:
the sudden rush of cars, the eccentricities of a nightingale:
her bronzed lips cracking for want of water.

Her dress slips from her shoulders; a rose tattoo,
a bright, dark memory of roses, sharp and sudden
as the needle that stitched his flesh into hers. *You,*

he writes in deepening shadows on her skin
are the clinging trellis that moves against the air,
rising like an angel, naked, eyes cast down.

My fingers weave red flowers through your fan of hair.
Father, she whispers, *I spread myself upon your bed of stone*
and your quickening breath is the only sound I hear.

Broken-Hearted Men

Evening finds the solitary man
hunched on his porch steps.
From the house of his nearest neighbour
Dean Martin rides
through an open door
from *loneliness to Tennessee*.
It was long ago
that he left the last party,
following the stars
as he stumbled home.

A boy's face looks up into his own,
an awful flower grew in his brain,
his outstretched hand touches the old separation
where once their hip-bones rubbed together.

The air has emptied itself of everything
human, and the last rose of the last summer
is faded and gone.

Soon, the streetcar will pull up beside him
and the bored conductor will ring the bell
as he pays for the ticket
that will take him forever, to the end
of the line, to his sweet-faced boy.
He is on his way home.

Bombshell

The red-headed G.I.'s favourite
unpins her elaborate plumage;
a scarlet carnage, the mind's

debacle. She discards
the metal clips on her dresser.
Her hairline was raised

fractionally, by electrolysis
leaving the high forehead
taut, deforested.

It was painful and slow
but she bore it patiently.
Her eyebrows were plucked

almost to extinction
then arched and shaded in
like history rewritten.

She is radiant, her smile
flaring over the white sands,
the blue, boiling ocean.

Once Upon A Time

There was a shy vibrant child who'd sit for hours
every day in the summer by the slow-moving river,
her mind cloudless, filled only with the gentle blues
and greens of her favourite season, with the rise
and fall of the golden sun to mark her mute
and blissful time. She'd watch the fishes glide by
underwater: sometimes they'd leap and arch
above the surface, and she was happy in the leafy
cathedral of silence. Then, one cloudless, gemlike
morning, she sat down sobbing, her small knees
tucked up under her chin. Her father had told her,
smilingly, at breakfast, of the house he'd bought
in a faraway city and her mother had nodded
with pleasure. *You need the company of other children,*
they'd told her kindly, *instead of sitting all day in the shade
of the trees and dreaming your dreams that can never be.*
Her tears dripped like fire-opals into the water, and a nearby
angel, shimmering and silver, perched gracefully on one
bowed shoulder. *Little one, what's breaking your heart?*
And she lifted her head and shyly told her. She finished
by crying, *I don't want to go. I want to stay here forever.*
And so you shall, said her delicate saviour, and twitching
her wings she turned the dreamer into a slender weeping-
willow that trailed its branches over the water, shading
the glittering swimmers, who although silent had always
loved her and wanted her there, above them, forever.

NOTE: *The Green River Killer was responsible for
the deaths of at least 49 women in Washington State
between 1982 and 1984. He was never caught.*

The river runs

The dumpsite, moss-choked, a riddle of bones
that wild animals have scattered and picked clean.
The graffiti, by an unknown hand, says *the river runs.*

The man on his raft in a glass-green afternoon
floats over car-wrecks, bottles and rusting cans
and a woman, fresh, the flesh still sticking to her bones

and before he can alter his course, another obstruction:
he pushes blindly with the wooden pole
through an overgrown land of bridges and trees.

A detective stumbles on the bank, the woman
sprawled out at his feet, this one alone
and he remembers the slaughterhouse downstream,

and the man with his half-finished cigarette,
bored and hot, looking down at another woman
in the polluted water, her face bloated,

her features wiped. Then the street-girls
with exotic names, idling in low-rent motels
before slipping into sequinned tops and skin-tight jeans

and strolling down the neon-lit strip
waiting for the one man who can take them away
from all this, to Star Lake, Maple Valley, Mount-View.

The bright tattoo of a tiger will fade
from Yvonne's exposed breast and the sun and rain
will unglue tight, painful braids, but the snake-design ring

will remain on the hand of black-haired Gisele
who was a blonde the last time anyone saw her,
before her head dipped quietly under the water.

Green River Rising

The women are marching
to reclaim the night: a candlelit
procession winds down the Sea-Tac Strip,
the cheap motels, rooms rented
by the hour, past the neon-lit
taverns, the cruising cars. They scan
the face of every driver.
They set out from the charred remains
of the burned-out slaughterhouse
where Dub Bonner and Wendy
rose from the water
that was never green, then
Marcia Chapman and Cynthia Hinds,
the mannequins that the raftsman
bumped, one sunny Sunday afternoon,
the rocks removed from their vaginas,
now tagged as evidence.
Then Amina Agisheff, mother of three
and snub-nosed Gisele Lovvorn,
young enough to be her daughter:
Denise Darcel who flipped the coin
that sent her out for cigarettes
she never bought. They found
her skull in Oregon, the rest of her
in Washington. Small hands hold
their struggling candles, blowing
in the chill Seattle wind. They
cannot speak, these women:
their necks raw from the makeshift
ligatures, their bodies aching
from the rapes when he pushed them
face down in the dirt, forcing
them deep into the darkness underneath,
covering them with branches
and dead leaves. Now, they're searching
for the ones the searchers didn't find:
Becky, April, Keli, Kase Ann Lee,

dark-eyed Marie. They'll search forever
till all forty-nine can join together
holding hands, mothers, daughters,
old friends. The women march on
out of sight.

Woman and Man

Down on my knees with a mouthful of flesh,
his damp, stubby fingers twitching in my hair
pushing my face down into his sweaty groin,
moaning *c'mon you bitch, I'm nearly there.*
You fuckhead. As if I really cared, my lips numb
from the rubber, my legs cramped and then,
finally his pathetic dribble of cum. *Is that all
you can manage mister?* I sit up, massaging
my aching jaw, making sure the dirty green
dollars are tucked safely into my pocket,
then I'll run for it. I'm outta here.
I look up at his vacant face. A derelict
shack, all boarded up. No one's home.
His eyes are weird. *Sick trick. Something's
wrong.* He's really quick. His pants are zipped.
He locks the door and cracks a hand
across my cheek. The handcuffs click
around my wrists. *He's done this before.
I'm not the first. Oh shit.* Then the odour
of something sweet, a rough cloth
across my face that makes my head spin.
I'm on the Strip, the red blue green flashing
of neon, the motel signs, cheap glass jewels
that light me through the scummy streets:
these dollar earrings that looked bright
as gold in the store, but bent all out
of shape and flaked and made my ears
bleed. I'm underwater, I'm flying high
looking blurrily down on the overgrown
lots, the silent streets. Then, like cheap
shoes *I don't know where I'm going
with this,* everything disintegrates.
I hear a jet roaring overhead. Fly away
big metal bird. Then silence.
The car's stopped. He's getting out.
I'm dragged like trash. Dark woods.
The branches whip my face. I taste
my blood. He lurches on, then

in a clearing shoves me down.
It's bloody cold out here. I should
be home. He's got my belt. What's
he doing with it? My throat is tight.
Can't breathe. Can't..............
Hey mister. You didn't pay for this.

Ugly on the Inside

Bitten-down nails dipped in *Gash*
by *Urban Decay*, lips smeared
with the same dark shade, as if
I'd sunk my teeth into my wrist
and come up smiling prettily.
My skin is grey, peeled from
the metal tray, my eyelids
brushed a deliberate red
and heavily lined in black.
A cut-throat razor's hack provides
a pulsing choker round my neck
with garnets that stain
my creased white dress: the unwanted
child rubbed over my face
demanding attention, refusing
to believe in its termination.
The CD growls its songs, the voice
of the dead girl from Seattle,
raped and strangled in an alleyway,
arms outflung like a crucifix.
I'll put her back in her plastic box.
This time I'll see she's silenced
forever. *Cut my skin and make me*
human. Tonight, I'll dance
into the early hours inside a church
that's now a club, and ignore midnight
and the shattering slippers
that cut my feet to scarlet ribbons.
I watch the honey-blonde
in her thigh-length, skin-tight dress,
her black heels, her swan's neck,
arched back, eyes dazzled by the lights.
She'll float downriver like a dream,
a princess, a homecoming queen.
Barefoot, I'll make my own way home,
make-up bleeding, my face askew,
through the darkened, narrow streets.

The Shy Stranger

It was a dark, green evening
in the porch's shade,
the taut tourniquet of ivy,

the slender wrists of spring,
the sun's late stain,
paint peeling like skin.

A girl stands up,
brushing her jeans,
leaving her twin
hunched over her notes
cramming for the last exam
oblivious of the departure
of the slender woman
who is carrying books
to the yellow car
for the shy stranger
with his arm in a sling.

She is carrying her body
to the Cascades
where it is lonely and cold,
where winter will shake
its bewildered head
over the ruins of her skull.

*

Journey

Bored by a journey that is taking forever,
watching the water sprawl beyond the horizon
I catch her tilted profile in the glass. At first
I mistake her for myself, half asleep
then I realise that these half-parted lips
aren't mine. A flash of jealousy. Then I want her:
closing my eyes, the sky-blue bedcovers flung back,
the windows wide open, our bodies shining
with morning sweat. Her drowsy face sinks back
onto the pillow, her spread legs twitch then fold
back together. I want to cup her face in my hands
and drown, going down together: her black hair drifting
back from her freckled pale skin, her body slipping water
down over the lovely bones of her shoulders, her breasts
fluid and darkly defined. Her arms are wrapped tightly
around my arched spine, our legs barely moving,
lungs filling as our eyes darken like twilight. The air
and the light are flaring into two huge and overblown roses.

School Reunion

There was never anything much to say
and what little there was has all been said.
I have sent all the untidy words away

to the sunlit schoolyard where they happily play
at whatever game comes into their heads.
There was never anything much to say

and the hallways are empty, the lists on display
of players, reserves, the missing, the dead.
I have shoved all the squabbling words away:

onto the sports-field where the sun hangs awkwardly
and a hockey-ball slaps my thigh, stinging red.
My stick pushes it out of play

and tiredly we file off, out of the day
to the showers, our shadows limping ahead.
I will scrub all the grime and harsh words away

rubbing my bruises, the purpling geography
of my clumsiness, a collision of heads.
(There was nothing that anyone could have said

to make it better.) The coach hands me the key
and remarks on the raggedness of the play.
To her, or to anyone, I have nothing left to say.
I lock the equipment and my stumbling words away.

Black Swan

An English garden, its lakes and lawns,
a corps de ballet of pale roses,
the drifting midwinter of swans.

She is lost in her shifting reflection.
The miniature bridge is stiffly arched
in its heavy slipper of stone.

Gone is the dark-haired, dark-eyed Russian
girl, bare-faced, black hair scraped back
from her aristocratic bones

who would sit mutely watching her swans.
Her breath tears at her throat
in a feverish spray of thorns.

In an empty theatre, the bouquets are strewn:
the elaborate costumes carefully hung
backstage in the many-mirrored room.

The sky darkens behind its stars.
The air is chilled. A frozen moon defines
the black swan rising from the lake.

Sailing off Cape Cod

She was mocked by his sisters
for her babykins voice, her shy whisper.
I don't talk any louder than this.

She grasped the tiller, guiding the yacht out
over the wind-ruffled water, turning
her head to smile at the Senator.

They sailed out farther than they'd ever meant,
weaving through a string of enchanted islands.
The mists sealed their eyes.

They struggled in its glistening nets.
A dazzling, white-sheathed woman
stepped out over the water,

snowflakes swirling around her dark head.
Her big face shone like a full moon.
She was in her element.

She thought she was alone on the yacht,
her companion had vanished beneath the waves.
A tiny baby was drowning beside its father.

A little girl was diving for pearls.
Before his hand touched her bare, cold shoulder
she saw the ghost ship and its ruined figurehead.

He'll Have to Go

I'm waiting in an empty restaurant
dressed up to the nines, but I might
be invisible or wearing another's face.
It feels later than it really is, and darker.

A cold, dark place. Our meeting-place
where you are always absent without apology.
That night I bought myself an hour's grace.
I've been paying for it ever since.

The food is cold. The plates are cracked.
Somewhere, a record I didn't ask for
begins to play. I am somewhere else.
You are at home, still sitting in that chair,

lost in your music while I search everywhere.
Four Walls. He'll Have to Go.
Father, I've sent all the boys away, and still
you won't come back to me.

The Mystery of the Missing Century
(for Gillian)

I stopped the car and stepped out onto gravel
being careful to grab my bag and lock the door.
I paused for half a minute to admire
the huge, overgrown gardens, the marble

statues, toppled or cracked or discoloured,
the woman who held a finger to her broken mouth
as if that might stop the secrets on her breath
from spilling out like leaves or water. I stopped,

I think, for more than half a minute.
I held my own breath, as somewhere a door
creaked open, then slammed shut like thunder.
I paused, out of caution, not fear, but my heart

took off at a gallop, my titian hair
streaming wildly in the wind which began
to rustle in the trees and soon outran
my heart which quietened down. I never

lost control in any situation: rule number one
and probably the most important one.

*

We are sailing on a charming bay,
all blue and gold and spilling
light. Bess leans back, lazily trailing
one hand through the fan-tailed spray

giggling at her distorted reflection.
I have a picture in my head,
another Bess, blonde, sweet and scared,
shivering as she crouches down

in an alley at the back of Hollywood.
The photographer stalks her
through the trash until she murmurs,
that's enough, goes back to bed.

The hidden bell will toll to warn
of water rising in the cave.
My pulse will quicken with each wave
as my sharp eyes swiftly scan

the darkness for a phantom, any phantom,
or the blank-faced drowning woman.
I no longer have the golden lines:
she'll have to save herself this time.

The blonde scrubs her face until it stings.
The photographer nervously hovers
wanting a caption for his pictures.
Call them the end of everything.

*

Jacqueline, you were a proud bay thoroughbred,
fine-boned, exotic, highly strung
with your father's wide-set dark eyes, circling
a circus-ring of Kennedys. Blue-blooded

girl, but practical, your father's little girl,
equestrienne with good, strong legs
and hands you thought were much too big,
not woman's hands, but what could spoil

these sleek, fine lines, the pink, full mouth
that valued silence, that kept its own
wise counsel. We had so much in common.
I wrote you after your father's death

expressing my heartfelt synpathy. I thought
that we might become friends, but your silence...
We each rode our own horses to the last fence.
You went to Dallas. I stayed in River Heights

avoiding that stampede: bullets and the bolting
horse, mouth raw from its see-sawing bit.
Pink-suited, blood-stained fashion plate.
Your legs flailed like a colt's, the car not stopping.

I reined my horse back from the drop.
The skies turned purple over Hyannisport.
You stand there in the bullet's acrid light
balancing a shy child against each hip.

*

I pull the book down from its place
on the dusty, sloping shelf.
I blow the dust into a face
mouthing words and mysterious shapes.

A swirl of snow, a momentary shiver,
the wind blows open the book's cover,
the sky, dark-blue, grey, well-thumbed,
the snow grubby with fingerprints.

The trees are no cover for anyone.
The wild-haired figure hides his face
in another, later page
where the puzzling footprints lead.

I settle down into an armchair to read
and feel ice-water flow through my heart's
creaking and uncarpeted space.

*

Nancy was a talented artist.
She sketched the face in profile,
head tilted, a ghost of a smile,
the smiling girl who is a ghost

of her former self. She deduces dates,
an autumn birth, a winter's death:
she walks her version of the earth
between these two fixed points

wearing down the thin plot.
She sinks deeper *into the valley
of the shadow of death*, her brown eyes
hooded, without light. The earth

is a bonfire now, eating the picture
of the smiling girl in Girl Scout uniform,
her elbow leaning casually on the chair arm,
the lamp unlit by her right shoulder

because outside it is early afternoon
and summertime and the sun shines.
The child in her believed that the sun shone
for her and her alone. Her, alone.

It was Nancy's greatest fear,
that of drowning, her slender
ankles caught in underwater debris
after her plane had nose-dived
into the ocean.
The window-glass that protected her
from the world would shatter her reflection
into the next, rudely, without warning.
She had never spoken to her father
about this, for fear of cracking
the charmed mirror of her existence.

How clear the weather was
when the plane lifted smoothly off,
how delphinium-blue the skies,
the sunlit faces of her two
excited passengers.
How quickly the fog descended.

*

Nancy imagined the scenes of mourning,
the red and blue flags at half-mast, the news
the world would awaken to: the loss of her light
aircraft over the Atlantic, as the terrible century
spiralled away from her.

Coastguard-cutters would retrieve the wreckage,
the broken body of their red-headed queen
still strapped into the cockpit, her classical
features intact, the torso and limbs
smashed up like stone: the rest of the plane
and her two lifelong friends scattered like shells
over the colourful bed of the ocean.

A little church in River Heights, crammed
with mourners for their mid-western girl
come home, the walls outside piled high
with blue larkspur and, this time,
a wire fence she couldn't wriggle through –
her disguise swept clean away, the pleading
glances and outstretched hands of old women:
white lilies, yellow roses, magazine pictures
with jagged edges, her faces wreathed in smiles.

Then finally, the flames, the oaken prison,
her body wrapped to look unbroken, her
beautiful face still smiling
as the titian flames broke down
the last secret door for her.

*

The space is cramped as one breath,
the little room that I have left,

up the twisting, sloping stairs,
through the unlocked oaken door

where the hooded figure studies a map
by the light of the study lamp:

night enmeshes the scaled-down plan.
He lifts a mansion in one hand

and shrinks to fit
leaving a tall, white candle-lit,

a pin-prick moving down the hall:
I have to squint to see at all.

The candle's pinched orange flame
narrows in the wind's half-rhymes.

*

I pull my flashlight from my purse,
or has the flashlight been lost already?
I can't remember. My light is unsteady
and anyway the attic is empty: a curse

from 1947, the black-eyed gipsy woman
with her tangled curls and common anger.
She drops my questions in the fire
and escapes behind her velvet curtains.

Light a candle for me father. The room is dark.
My fingers read the walls like braille
except there's nothing to be read at all.
I follow the stony trail, each sudden crack

as if the walls were opening as I speak.
I press and knead, I push and tap
as if a secret panel might slide up
or back or to one side and I might break

myself back into the well-worn story
where no mere man-made trap can hold me,
and I step out into the disused pantry
or grab the coiling gift of ivy

which twists and drips its dark green wax
down the brickwork, from its flame
where the sun pours upwards from
the tiny window – Jack in the Box,

its endless golden grin, bursting through
the afternoon: I read the omens as they came,
the sinister black bird from last night's dream
but I must have blinked and missed the final clue.

*

Memoirs

Dear father, in your library you sit
at your desk of battered mahogany
with its relics of a brighter time,
its fine old lines, a map
of broken words and scorings-out.

The wine glass is a rich, red light,
a plum plucked from the glistening
tree of night, its wild silhouette
dancing lightly outside the window.
Long, nervous fingers glide
across the wooden sheen like ships
drifting out of sight, in a mist
quite unforeseen, sailing
above a bed of wrecks.

The gold-nib of your fountain pen
scratches over a book of stone,
scratches idly like a cat,
suffused with blood-light.

Queen Victoria's Painting

*Asked about the tale of the 'Anastasia' who had somehow
dodged the bullets and escaped to the West, Nikulin replied
in the flat, simple diction of one who knew.
    'They all perished,' he said.*

Princess Alice is playing Chopin's Funeral March
with a melancholy, delicate touch
as her child's hands push at the window-latch.
Blood seeps through his brain like a summer storm.
Black shadows sweep across the sun
as he is lifted up from the paving-stones.

Diphtheria is spreading through the royal household.
She strokes her eldest son's feverish face
as she explains that his sister May has gone
to join little Frittie in heaven.
She bends down to let him kiss her.

The remaining children watch in silence
as her coffin is carried out to the chapel.
It will soon be Christmas and the snow
should glitter and swing like a rope
of jewels as the wind waltzes down
the long avenue of trees; but today
the ballroom is dark and empty.
Their clothes and toys have been burned.

The widowed English Queen sits in the garden
at Darmstadt in her mourning weeds
trying to paint little Alix,
dear, beautiful Alix who won't be still.
Paint drenches the canvas.
The heat has drained her.
The little dancing girl is making her dizzy:
the same blood rushes through their veins.
This is no longer her painting:

this pit in a clearing in a forest
dug at night-time by a band of soldiers,
the stifling hot engineer's house
with its whitewashed windows, firmly latched
against which Frittie's determined ghost
can hurl himself to no avail,
where in a basement room with two chairs
a family and their servants will gather.
Here, Alix will make the sign of the cross.
It will be an incomplete gesture.
Life here is nothing, she will have written
in a letter to a friend. Her faith was strong.

Her children will be orphans for a matter
of minutes. Their clothes and possessions
will be burned. The following night, their
bodies will be moved for a second time.
Then it will all be over.

The Empress Dreams in Miniature

a spring afternoon
at the end
of the century   a simple
wooden cross
in dirt
a tiny chapel
that the sun
strikes   a clock
opens   a man
steps out
leaves flowers
on the earth   staring
at nothing before
crossing himself
the sun   cold gold
unhinged   spilling
the day
in miniature

the gold
springs open   she
shrinks back
into herself   bare
boards   outside
the dawn
call of birds
drowned by the restless
engine   her heart
stopped   the miniature
firing squad with golden
rifles and bayonets
the needle's
sting   a ruby
drop of blood swelling
like a heart   her
husband slumped

a broken
marionette   his blood
winding through
her veins   a window
cracked   her daughters
swaying dressed
as peasants for
charades and afterwards
the soldiers stripping
away their rags
spilling gems
that deflected death
until the glass
broke   the bayonets
piercing flesh
between the sapphire
sky the emerald
earth   soaked
blood overflowing
the egg cracked

sweat-drenched
she awoke   a familiar
room   her hands
crossed   outside
the sun
slipping into dark
earth   the clock
striking
the century beginning
the end

The House of Special Purpose

This is only a game. We are children playing.
The lift is descending
towards the brightly lit basement
where my playmates are waiting
holding hands, a wreath of roses
in the centre of their circle.
It is too soon I try to tell them
but already they are weaving me into their pattern
with the needle pushed down into a vein.

I am Grand Duchess Anastasia,
the youngest daughter of the Tsar
although the nurses have called me Fraulein Unbekannt
since I was hauled unconscious from a Berlin canal.
I have no family willing to acknowledge me.
As the bullets ricocheted off the walls of the cellar,
the truck, outside, in the garden, was revving its engine.
My sisters were still standing and the soldiers
were becoming hysterical. They thought that I was dead
until I sat up on the makeshift stretcher and screamed.

I am growing tired of this game. I have climbed
to an attic with one high, tiny window
from which light falls like a bayonet
upon the uneven boards, the useless icons,
the trunks stuffed full of dolls, their faces
porcelain, their glassy blue eyes winking.
There will be a secret panel where the wall sounds hollow.
This is where we part, my little shadow.

The lift is moving up one final floor.
Already I am yawning and restless
and I can only remember my own name.

Each Perfect Girl

The models stumble, knee-deep in winter, their bare legs
burnished gold and blue like precious chains.
Their ankles twist sharply with every step, pitching them
forward, out of the ragged fringes of forest.

The moon beams down on rows of skinny editors
swathed in black, gripping their little folding chairs,
their eyes following each swaying limb, wobbling
on its perilous heel. Red, green, gold and blue gowns

swirl like snow around each perfect girl.

The Winter Collections

The dead stroll down the marble runways of Milan.
Children clutch their programmes and applaud.
A sturdy, smiling man swings round:
his black leather coat twirls of its own accord.
His girls are a shimmering column, each bird
or insect more dazzling than the last. He grabs
an ocean-drenched wing, pressing it tenderly to his chest.

Now we have a cathedral, a requiem mass,
the small, intense man mouthing his words,
hands raised, spinning, blowing a kiss
into a scissored flurry of crimson swatches
scattered over the marble steps.

Ophelia's Confession

Every day God pats my head and calls me
angel, his little broken woman
and gives me flowers as if I hadn't had enough of these
and I choke back my rage and he mistakes this
for distress as I stand there shaking
in my little sackcloth dress.

Had I ever had the choice
I'd have worn a very different dress,
slit from breast to navel and far too tight
and I'd have smoked and sworn and been
out of my head on drugs, not grief, and the flowers
would have been a tattoo around my ankle,
not an anchor to drag me down, and as for
being a virgin, I'd have slept with both men and women.

I would never recommend a shallow stream
and what was no more than a daisy chain
as being the ideal way to die.
It was far too pretty but I had to improvise
and I was a poet, far more so than him,
who threw out every word he ever thought
as if that might have kept his sorry life afloat.

I didn't drown by accident. I was a suicide.
At least let me call my mind my own
even when my heart was gone beyond recall.

Today, a car crash might have been my final scene,
a black Mercedes in a tunnel by the Seine,
with no last words, no poetry,
with flashbulbs tearing at my broken body
because broken was the way I felt inside,
the cameras lighting up the wreckage of a life.
That would, at least, have been an honest way to die.

The Last Photo-Opportunity

Did I really look that bored? That stuck-up?
I suppose I must have done, but did you
never think to put your paints and brushes
back in your bag and to ask me what was wrong?
Did it never occur to you that I might have been in pain?
Cast your mind back. It was actually quite cold
and the sky threatened rain and my dress
was very thin and left my arms and neck quite bare.
I was freezing, covered in flowers, singing
snatches of my favourite songs, very badly,
and I mean, what did you... oh never mind.

I suppose I should be grateful that you didn't ask me
to hitch up my dress, rearrange my carelessly
draped flowers, to hold that pose a little longer, although
whether I'd have heard you is open to question.
But I should be grateful to you for these small things.
After all, I had such little time left to myself by then.

The Gardener

The rake scrolls its claw across the lawn,
slippery-wet from the morning's deluge:
jade dragon, guardian of the mishapen,
collector of leaves and small stones.

It is rewriting its obsessive scrawl;
days of work to no end.

The gardener is silent and thinking in pictures,
a gallery of bare trees and stopped fountains.
Once the words were easy, now they drip
like a cistern onto damp flagstones
in a dark outhouse where nobody goes.
He has been over this ground before.

A World With Only One Song

The black disc and my world is spinning.
The needle jumps sideways back to the beginning.
The sun, that blinding, great composer
has rolled the day right over.

My heart is a tree, cut clean through.
The woodman has ripped it from the heart of you.
The forest is a single tree.
A ring of mirrors reflects it to infinity.

My mind has scattered all its seeds
and the trail is bare and my heart bleeds.
My heart and my hands are empty now
and no green seeds will ever grow

up into the sky where Jack can climb
and lose himself in perfect time,
and the giant will snap the fragile stalk
and weeds will choke the healing clock

and when the hands grind to a halt
I will descend into the starless vault
that was my heart, and find the clue
that will lead me, at last, away from you.

The steps lead down and down and down.
There has only ever been one song,
each note swallowed by the carrion birds.
You and I have lost the words.

The Ruins

I roll each unfamiliar word around
on a broken tongue, grown too huge for my mouth,
a river thick with rotting flowers,
a disintegrating cloak of pollen.
Memory fails me like a snapped branch,
my skirt swells with water, my sackcloth lungs.
My limbs and my tongue have turned to stone:
I speak in tongues, garbled and draughty.
How could we have missed each other?
Only one door, but a mockery of exits and entrances.

I kiss your face through dark tears,
through the veils that swarm like bees
or charred flowers weaving their heavy scents
into a rope to squeeze the breath from me.

I move idly in the breeze, letting my keys dig
a row of shallow graves along each finger.
The old, bloody river is overflowing its banks:
the cold waves wash me out to sea again.

A knife is pulled from its rusting sheath:
the fat, bumbling father clutches
the velvety bellies of his curtain,
babbling about how he tucked my face
into the huge, scarred spaces of his heart.
The night is breezy. The news of your death
soon dries to a vermilion scream,
a shrivelled zero. I reach out a hand
to touch the glassy air, tilting
and emptied of everything.
See what I've hoarded for this rainswept
evening, the broken furniture
and dust sheets. Utter penury.
My broom has swept the garden bare.

I hold out both my hands to you.
They are blue as the sky with the cold
and as bruised and as far away as love.
I think of the patient, starless dark,
the airy corridors and winding stairways
of healing, where we might finally touch.

Leaving the Enchanted City

1

She lays aside the pencil-sketch she has finished
and framed, of the city she loves.
Its streets wind through her heart.
They are squeezing her breathless.
The day is too busy and too hot.
She wipes her handprints from the glass.

Hours of tentative lines and erasure
will realign the days, although the nights
are sleepless and cracked:
red-eyed digits flash on the clock.
She walks through each room reaching for shadows,
swinging them up into her arms.

A door slams, slipping from her hand.
His face escapes her as she turns around
another corner. She has been
to every address: black railings rise
out of the ground, framing dolls-house lawns.
She steps over the broken faces of strangers.

A train is flying above the river
stretching out over the iron hump
of the bridge: the evening sun
has found a quiet hollow to play in
on the smooth side of a hill. The sky smears
its blue paints brightly over each window.

On the lawn below her is a girl,
her arms folded over her stomach.
The man beside her is taciturn.
The flowers are rich and full.
It is summer, after all, and the city
has hollowed a place for her in its heart.

2

Without her, the world is perfectly balanced
and lyrical: the careful placing
of trees, streets, buildings, the wide
stone bridge, a red bus stopped
and just visible over the bridge's curve.
The light is angled and rolling
like a wheel. She has stepped
outside for air, emerging
where the world is loose and clear, hanging
from its taut white line.

She has taken a vow of silence
and stretches like a cat on her stomach
in the grass below the castle's shadow.
Her shadow is climbing the rock, freewheeling.
Now she has left the enchanted city

and crossed the wide, blue river.
It is evening, late June, and the world shines.
The gasworks are fat pillars of salt.
If she looked back now, she would turn to stone
but the sun, the sun warms everything.

3

The ponies are a charmed circle of bronze,
lurid, stamping standing-stones.
The day is toppling around them.
Their tails flicker, their haunches gleam.

The steeplechaser crumples on impact,
his body, a broken shape in the wet grass.
He was jumping shadows as the golden frame
of evening sunlight tilted over the winding river.

The train holds the coast close.
Walking across the water would bring us
full circle. Back to the beginning.

4

The evening light is cognac,
restful in its black glass.
The city is a gold-scrolled tray
piled with lights and lifted smoothly,
shoulder-high, by a silent
white-gloved waiter.

There are monuments everywhere:
a giant horse steps gracefully
out from the dark. His ears
are pricked, the tips as sharp
as swords. His rider is perfectly
focused, his thoughts,
once as scattered as the stars,
now drawn together.

She is walking uphill,
always moving forwards
before the nervous look back over
her shoulder, sparing herself
nothing: the bold, black lines,
brilliant lighting, the twisting designs
laid out before her like a map
that has grown nightmarishly in her shrinking hands;
the city with its spires and its shadows cast
by the spires and serrated towers,
its cold, blank spaces and its white-faced clocks.

5

She holds the glass up
to her face, then lowers it,
stepping into her broken reflection,
slipping out of herself.
Her feet are paddling in a warm sea,
her skirt pushed up over her hips.

The Forth is tilted:
water in a shallow glass,
the irritant of an island,
a distant ship, tall
chimneys on the vanishing coast.

Roads lead off like the points of a star.

The sky is very close:
her fingers claw at the scattered clouds,
its cold, blue face.
The water is light and clear.
It ripples under her back.
The breeze is fresh.

Long ago, when she was a child,
she dreamed this.

A Book of Favourite Horse Stories

When she was twelve, she unwrapped the book of horses
he'd brought back from a business-trip:
not just a book, but the lush and rolling earth
and all the majestic horses on it;
Citation, Secretariat and Man O'War
whose twenty-eight foot stride ate up the gallops,
but the wild-eyed white stallion
that she tried to coax out from its pages
couldn't be driven by even the most ardent
imagination. It flattered to deceive, a morning glory
which would spend its days being pushed out
along one thousand finishing-straights
a hundred lengths behind the winner,

leading her here, along the narrow paths
of this small-town cemetery, genteel and dusty,
unremarkable, a main road passing the main-gates
which were low enough to scramble over
even without an Arkle or an Easter Hero.
She'd removed the sweat-soaked tack long ago
and bolted the failure into its stable,
nailing the doors shut with a plaque
testifying to his modest parentage,
his ill-health, his underachievements,
and now all that remained was the stone,
her unacknowledged failings harnessed
to his own. She'd realised, too late,
as she was pulling up, after passing the elusive
finishing-post, that he might have given all that he could.

God's Drawing

Dark brown wood,
polished and fluid,
bones sliding
like pistons
through silk-clasped
muscles: sweat
deepens each hair
to mahogany.
Black tassels twitch
against a hum of flies.

This is the hard graft
of centuries, the answer
to the final equation:
old men poring over
dry, spidery bloodlines
or maybe God simply
drew you from memory.

Back now to the green
that gives with the ease
of breathing under
your iron feet, the legs
as brittle as sticks, tongue
pink and thick, hanging
over the bit's restraint.

I know this by heart –
the way you'll break out
of the gate, then settle
as quietly as a child
sleeping, then the white-
splashed face leading
the field around
the tight turns
of Tattenham Corner
these bit-part players
who might be in
another country:

and out of the corner
of one white-rimmed eye,
you catch the crowds
dressed for another century.
You've slipped your bridle,
your rider, the day:
ghost horse,
you left the world here.

Racing Bronze

This horse weighed little in the sculptor's hands:
his whirling fingers ploughed the neck's rough furrows
where fresh air now weaves and the mane lies
heavy as a river clogged by solid gold.

He worked from a photograph of the arrogant
god, posed idly in his 1930s stable-yard,
reins slung loosely over taut, muscled shoulders.
The stable-lad is missing from the picture.

Other heads hang over wooden doors and blow
hotly into the dead summer afternoon where
leaves twitch lazily like the ears of horses.
The breeze feints and darts in and out

of trees that darkly frame the yard.
Anchored by his bronze hooves to the plinth,
his head is raised, he seems about to move.
His silence is skittish with light.

Lyric Fantasy

The taut muscles
of lightly raced fillies,
a paddock of vibrant green

washed by the early
morning rain, the cool
sponge of spring;

an alert freshness
of horses,
the spirited scribble

of heads and manes,
billowing silks,
lyrical, indelible

as weather,
the colours of kingfishers,
chessboards, angels.

Not even the clouds
have anything less
than classic pretensions,

elegiac above the slender
parade of trees
and horses circling.

One Thousand Guineas for a Queen

(a winner's corona, for John)

Honey light bathes a parade of fillies,
these fleet-footed girls of spring
whose humble duty is to run.
Their fairy footsteps mark the afternoon.

Flying water skims a bed of pebbles
beneath the witch-elm, in the sunstream
where exhibitionists kick up elegant heels
in farewell to this dancing time.

Petite étoile, sceptre, diadem,
make picture play around the silver urn
where the wheel of fortune picks one name.
Here, Charlotte became the belle of all

and cherry lass performed with flair.
Sun chariot rode the tranquil air
above the briar-root, the happy laughter.
One thousand guineas for a queen.

Some mangled Dream Songs for Henry who is twenty-eight years dead and past caring.

1

Shadowed by your father
in his terrible pose, the shotgun crammed
into his mouth, and inside the house
the bewildered little boy who heard
the echo of that shotgun blast
through every dawn that ever rose

far off in the reddening east.
As each bright morning rises
your lover's face turns briefly
on the crumpled pillow, her cheeks warm,
her sweet, delicious lips, pouting
and closed just like a morning rose.

Yes, you'll ruin her too, tear her root and limb
from the soil that nourishes her,
and try to cram her in the glass
that sits clearly on your window-sill,
cursing when her sharp claws scratch you
and crying like a little boy

when night comes and she's gone back home.

2

A ragged mob with bayonets,
revolvers, orders from a higher source,
might as well have lined you up
in some cramped room. A chair for Delmore
who could barely stand, and Sylvia,
the youngest one and then the farce
                 of ricocheting bullets, bayonets

and the waiting lorry that the villagers
would pretend not to hear,
then stretchers carried out
into the night, up from the cellar
into the silent house, leaving the punched-
out plaster walls to crumble –

then the acid vats, the stripping
of the clothes, the treasure troves
of images sewn into their linen hiding place.
Think of all these poems burned
along with flesh and better times.
Bye bye to immortality then,

Henry. Are you listening
to me?

3

Then some fool poet would be born
who'd stand one day on the empty earth
where the massacre had taken place
and write of bones found in dark woods
and lay her sheaf of wilting flowers
upon the ground and say a prayer

whose meagre words would be ripped up
by the chill, Russian air
whilst a man in a buttoned-up black coat
would drop his shabby bundle too
and bow his head and cross his heart
and think of the four laughing daughters

chopped down well before their time
in a cellar, in a house torn down
but still the bare earth provides a shrine,
one wooden cross, a tiny platform
that could be a poet's stage
for we're all actors, bad or good

caught between Caesar, the shuffling fool,
Ophelia in her stinking pool.

4

The stacks of books, tidily arranged
with their red-haired heroine
who innocently pokes around
and hunts the evil villains down
and who is always kept quite safe
from the rapist's knife,

the mother who hated her from birth,
the scald of water on her breast,
the scarlet handprints on her thighs,
the adolescent overdose, the senseless note,
written in green eyeliner, mispelt,
thrown away and never read.

She's better now. She's made it past
your generation's youngest ghost.
She likes to read and some nights
she can even sleep. She eats
what's put in front of her, with gratitude
and sometimes finds the time to write

a word or two, although she'll tilt
her head modestly and say she'll
never be half as good as you.
She is *the little girl who smokes*
and smokes (here, I've changed a word),
but red pens aren't found in the grave

and so I'm quite safe in misquoting you.
She is the little girl who knows better.
Not much.

5

So little Anna has her pills that numb
and make her cold, unable to come
in the arms of any man, especially
the man she loves and cannot have
for isn't that the way of love,
the ways of love that make you numb

until the ghostly father comes
and reminds her that she has a heart
that beats and a complex clock of parts,
that she is more than just mere bones
with tissue and veins neatly sewn
under the skin that can't keep warm.

In his chest, she can hide her face
and cry her tears, and not wish
to be any other place but there.
He'll dry her tears and stroke her hair
and she'll turn her finely contoured face
into his, with tenderness.